The Xenophobe's® Guide to The Americans

Stephanie Faul

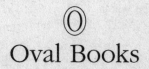

Oval Books

Published by Oval Books
335 Kennington Road
London SE11 4QE
United Kingdom

Telephone: +44 (0)20 7582 7123
Fax: +44 (0)20 7582 1022
E-mail: info@ovalbooks.com
Web site: www.xenophobes.com

First published by Ravette Publishing, 1994
Reprinted 1995,1996,1997,1998

First published by Oval Books, 1999
Reprinted 2000; updated 2001

Editor – Catriona Tulloch Scott
Series Editor – Anne Tauté

Cover designer – Jim Wire, Quantum
Printer – Cox & Wyman Ltd
Producer – Oval Projects Ltd

Xenophobe's® is a Registered Trademark.

Acknowledgement and thanks are given to
McDonald's Restaurants Ltd for their kind
permission to use their product on the cover.

Author's dedication: This work is dedicated
to Frances Trollope, who in 1832 published
a much better book on the same subject.

ISBN: 1-902825-16-0

Contents

The American population is 275 million (compared with 31 million Canadians; 49 million English; 92 million Mexicans; 125 million Japanese; 148 million Russians; and 1.2 billion Chinese).

Nationalism and Identity

Forewarned is Forearmed

Americans are like children: noisy, curious, unable to keep a secret, not given to subtlety, and prone to misbehave in public. Once one accepts the Americans' basically adolescent nature, the rest of their culture falls into place, and what at first seemed thoughtless and silly appears charming and energetic.

Visitors may be overwhelmed by the sheer exuberant friendliness of Americans, especially in the central and southern parts of the country. Sit next to an American on an airplane and he will immediately address you by your first name, ask "So – how do you like it in the States?", explain his recent divorce in intimate detail, invite you home for dinner, offer to lend you money and wrap you in a warm hug on parting.

This does not necessarily mean he will remember your name the next day. Americans are friendly because they just can't help it; they like to be neighbourly and want to be liked. However, a wise traveller realises that a few happy moments with an American do not translate into a permanent commitment of any kind. Indeed, permanent commitments are what Americans fear the most. This is a nation whose most fundamental social relationship is the casual acquaintance.

How They See Themselves

As befits a nation originally settled by misfits, convicts, adventurers, and religious fanatics (a demographic mix that has changed hardly at all in 400 years), the United States retains a strong flavour of intransigent non-co-operation. Americans are proud to be American – it's the best country in the world – but each individual will explain that he, personally, is not like other Americans. He is better. Americans are proud to be different from each other, and from the world. As a nation of immigrants, they can be of any global ethnicity, that Americans are likely to have had their teeth straightened.

There's no such thing as a plain American, anyway. Every American is a hyphenated-American. The original 'melting pot' has crystallised out into a zillion ethnic splinters: Croatian-Americans, Irish-Americans, Japanese-Americans, Mexican-Americans, and so on. A typical American might introduce him or herself as Patrick Ng, Octavio Rosenberg, or Ilse-Marie Nugumbwele.

An American will say "I'm Polish" or "I'm Italian" because his great-grandparents were born in Poland or Italy. It doesn't matter that he speaks not a word of any language besides English and has never been farther east than New York City or farther west than Chicago. He knows how to make kolatches (if he's Polish) or cannelloni (if he's Italian), and that's what counts.

A spirit of rugged individualism pervades virtually every aspect of American life. Americans' heroes are outlaws, like wild west gunfighter Jesse James, or entrepreneurs, like Sam Walton, founder of the Wal-Mart chain of superstores. Their ogres are totalitarians of every stripe, including communists, presidents of major corporations, law officers and politicians. Every American worker has fantasies of one day going into business for himself. Individualism extends even to matters domestic: nearly one-third of American households consist of only one person.

How They See Others

Only 20% of Americans own passports. They don't need them. An American can travel for a week and still be on home turf. The fact that everyone who lives within 3,000 miles of an American is also an American gives the average citizen a seriously provincial point of view. Because Americans visit foreign countries relatively seldom*, they assume that people all over the world are just like themselves, except for not speaking English or having decent showers.

Some Americans believe that foreign natives really do speak English (they study it in school, you know), but refuse to do so out of prejudice. The delusion that 'they're just like us except for their language, food, and clothing' comes from the reality that nearly all Americans descend from foreign immigrants. Thus people in other countries aren't really aliens, they're just potential Americans, or rather, potential hyphenated-Americans.

Special Friends

Americans have a special relationship with Canadians, with whom they share the world's longest undefended border. In fact, most Americans aren't fully aware that Canada is a separate sovereign nation. Canadians look and talk like Americans, and the Toronto Blue Jays won the World Series baseball championship. Any champion baseball team must be from the United States, no matter what its supporters think.

Europe is not very well differentiated in the American mind. American travellers on guided tours happily swing through five countries in seven days, returning home with the vague notion that the Eiffel Tower is somewhere in the neighbourhood of the Tower of Pisa – which, by American standards, it is. The distance from London to Istanbul is less than the distance between Pittsburgh and Phoenix and only two-thirds the mileage from Maine to Miami.

* Canada doesn't count.

Americans feel sentimental about England. They import much of their decent literature and most of their better television programmes from Britain, and anyone over 50 worships the country that produced the Beatles and the Rolling Stones. There's also the Royal Family element: lacking a domestic equivalent, Americans lap up the latest imported blue-blooded scandals. Royal weddings attract huge American audiences, who sigh at the glorious un-American pomp of it all.

By contrast, the Japanese are distrusted because they are everything the Americans are not: group-oriented, sexist, conformist and ethnically monotonous. The fact that a great many Japanese are richer than they are doesn't bother them at all.

Character

Like every other nation, America knows that it's the best country in the world. The difference is that Americans have proof: people from all over the globe make enormous sacrifices to come to the United States, often risking their lives in the process. What more evidence is needed?

Being Number One is very important to an American. In the United States, it's definitely not how you play the game that matters. It isn't even really whether you win or lose. It's whether you look like you win or lose – more specifically, win. Winning is central to the American psyche. As American football coach Vince Lombardi put it, "Winning isn't everything. It's the only thing". Virtually every event in American life, from school graduation to marriage to buying an automobile, is structured so that one party wins, or at least comes out looking better than any of the other participants.

What is more, Americans believe themselves to be the only nation that is truly capable of winning. They are always being called in at the last minute to bail some backwater nation out of the soup. Having God on your side in a fight is good. Having the United States on your side is better. To an American, they're the same thing.

Once the battle is over and negotiations begin, however, Americans change from warriors into wimps. As humourist Will Rogers put it, "America never lost a war and never won a conference in our lives. I believe that we could, without any degree of egotism, single-handedly lick any nation in the world. But we can't confer with Costa Rica and come home with our shirts on."

The Feel-Good Factor

Winning is important to Americans because it makes them feel good, and good is the American thing to feel. Americans spend thousands of dollars on books, drugs, and various forms of psychotherapy in order to feel good. The most widely prescribed psychiatric drug in the country is an anti-depressant. Americans attend therapy groups, participate in self-discovery retreats, experience 'primal scream therapy' and 'rebirthing', and so forth. (Much of this activity takes place in California, the feel-good state.)

The American reaction to any kind of disaster or crisis is to feel good about it. Americans always look at the bright side, whether or not there is one, and if possible accentuate the positive of every disaster. "If life hands you lemons, make lemonade", they'll chirp as they examine the smashed wreck of their car or the earthquake-ravaged ruin of their house; "I always hated that kitchen."

Feel-goodism affects all aspects of private and public life. Universities hand out academic awards to anyone with even a passable performance. The American business world is full of rosy projections and enthusiastic estimates. The government and various associations hand out awards and citations for excellence like so many Christmas cards. It's a rare American who doesn't have on his wall at least one Certificate of Excellence, whether in Management, Salesmanship, or Best Attitude.

Every American bookshop has shelves and shelves of self-help books. Titles such as *I'm OK, You're OK*; *Feeling Good: The New Mood Therapy*, and *The Seven Habits of Highly Effective People*, an incomprehensible field guide for success-seeking business people, top the nation's bestseller lists. The *New York Times Book Review* gives such books their own bestseller list so they won't crowd out the real books.

Elementary schools focus on teaching children self-esteem, urging them to feel good about their accomplishments (even if such accomplishments don't include the ability to perform long division without a calculator). Some schools have stopped giving spelling tests because many of the children couldn't get all the words right and the resulting failure damaged their confidence, i.e., made them feel bad.

Insecurity

The dark side of American cheerfulness is the undercurrent of insecurity and depression that drives much of the country's commerce and nearly all of its psychiatry. Underneath their grins, Americans are deeply fearful, pessimistic, and unhappy. They're afraid that after working so hard, someone – whether the government through taxes or a thief through force – will take the things they value away from them.

Americans feel inadequate to meet life's challenges.

They're afraid they will lose their jobs. They're afraid their children will grow up to become criminals, pornographic film stars, or, worse still, politicians. They're afraid that eating raw oysters will kill them, that their neighbours make more money than they do, that they have cancer.

If they are single they're afraid they will never get married, if married they're afraid they will get divorced, if divorced they fear they will never meet anyone attractive ever again. To prevent these dire events Americans move to the suburbs, install car alarms, buy insurance, avoid shellfish, go into therapy, join clubs for singles, and see marriage counsellors. Often this only makes the anxiety worse by bringing sufferers into contact with people who have the same problem.

Being depressed is unattractive and thus not suitable for public display. The preferred reaction is treatment, either with drugs or psychotherapy or both, and concealment. If pressed about his or her state of mind an American will admit, "Oh, I've been depressed for a while, but I feel pretty good about it now."

When seeing each other off on a journey, Americans will say "Have a safe trip". The travellers will have updated their wills and made sure the insurance is current, because you never know what can happen. You *do* know it probably won't be good.

It's a Conspiracy

Americans see conspiracies behind every event, from the Kennedy assassination to the worldwide spread of AIDS. After all, things don't just happen by chance, do they. Someone must be pulling the strings.

Who really runs the world? A conspiracy, obviously. Opinions differ as to whether it involves the Illuminati or the Trilateral Commission, or possibly the Catholic church, but the underlying paranoia remains the same.

But That Was Last Week

In some countries, disgraced politicians kill themselves. In America they run for office. The American public has a short collective memory and easily forgives a sinner. Thus, Richard Nixon, the only US president ever to resign under threat of impeachment, became an elder statesman in his later years on the strength of his China policies. Marion Barry, the mayor of Washington, DC, was jailed for drug use in 1989. Four years later he ran for his old office and was elected by a safe margin. One mayor of Boston was re-elected while he was in jail. In Florida, Judge Alcee Hastings was removed from office for corruption by the US Congress. His home town promptly elected him as a representative to that august body.

Behaviour

Family Values

Conservative politicians in particular like to natter on about family values. The problem is that in America nobody is exactly sure what that means. The divorce and illegitimacy rates are high, homosexual couples are having and adopting children in greater numbers, and nearly a third of Americans live alone anyway.

Marriage in the United States tends to look more like serial monogamy than lifetime partnership, especially in the major cities. Just under half of all marriages end in divorce. However, this statistic is misleading: many people, such as Elizabeth Taylor Hilton Wilding Todd Fisher Burton Burton Warner Fortensky, marry repeatedly, but three-quarters of Americans who marry for the first time stay that way. The others go through several spouses before settling down. And approximately 10% of men and 6% of women never marry at all.

When Americans say 'family', they mean a nuclear family of Mom, Dad, and the kids. That such households are melting down at a prodigious rate doesn't affect the cultural ideal one iota.

Another component of the ideal family is a non-working wife, the caring, nurturing mother who greets children after school with a plate of home-baked cookies. Such women, while they do exist, are nearly extinct. More than 80% of women between the ages of 35 and 45 are employed outside the home for the simple reason that they need the money. The children go to day care nurseries or stay with a relative or neighbour; when they're old enough, they go to school and to after-school care. Working parents, especially those in demanding careers, must console themselves by spending 'quality time' rather than quantity time with their children.

Children are raised to be independent and cautious, with a strong sense of self-esteem. American parents treat their children with a near-deference unheard of in most European households: "Would you like Froot Loops or Captain Crunch for breakfast? Is that enough milk? OK, I'll put it into the teddy bear bowl instead." Child culture, in the person of Big Bird and Barney the Dinosaur, invades the home and takes over the conversation and the television, and child activities dominate evenings and weekends. Homework is often minimal, so the children have plenty of time to watch television.

It is difficult and expensive for parents to get a baby-sitter because local teenagers are probably working at McDonald's. Thus American parents take their children to all sorts of functions such as cocktail parties, the cinema and weddings.

Children are raised in as risk-free a manner as possible. Along with his or her first bicycle, an American child also receives a safety helmet. The government continually tests toys to make sure they can't cause harm even when used inappropriately; gone are the days of home chemistry sets and slingshots. School athletics has switched from American football to the less violent soccer, while insurance liability has removed high-diving boards from community pools.

On the other hand, in many areas teenagers are given a car as soon as they are old enough to drive (usually 16). The insurance payments are astronomical, but since there's little public transportation it saves hours every day for mothers. Such cosseted, protected children grow up into perfect Americans – self-centred, self-assured, competent, cheerful, and eager to try something life-threatening now that their parents are finally off their backs.

The Perpetual Teenager

For many Americans the best years of their lives were in high school – the years between 15 and 18. Teenagers have few responsibilities, plenty of disposable income, and lots of energy with which to have fun and get into trouble. Americans never outgrow this stage, continuing to indulge themselves and dodge responsibility right into senility.

Given his choice, the American man wants to be a sports star like basketball wonder Michael Jordan or football quarterback Joe Montana. (It doesn't hurt that both these gentlemen are rich.) You can see weekend athletes on playgrounds all across the country, shooting baskets and pretending they could have gone professional if they hadn't had to earn a living.

American women yearn to be film stars or models, and spend their weekends shopping for cosmetics to make them look like Cameron Diaz or Tyra Banks. They also yearn for a domestic fantasy, and dream about redecorating the guest bathroom, making needlepoint chair-covers, and 'putting up' quarts of home-canned tomatoes. Martha Stewart, a television personality with her own magazine, has earned a fortune telling American women how to iron their sheets, grow their own salads, and make dried flower wreaths. Virtually no women actually do these things. For many Americans, fantasising about their own potential is a full-time activity.

Sex

Whatever kind of sex it is they're having, Americans know that it could be better. Books about improving one's sex life top the sales charts, and women's magazines in particular feature at least one How to Have Better Sex article every month. Nowadays it's OK to be open about sex.

But being open isn't the same thing as being relaxed. Americans retain a strong prudish streak. Public nudity is illegal in most states, and at the beach bathers wear suits that provide at least a minimum of decency, particularly men, who wear shorts that contain three times the amount of fabric in the average European swimsuit. Topless and nude beaches are rare, and going topless at a public beach makes one subject to arrest. (On the other hand, women in New York City have won the right to ride the subway topless if they so choose.)

Adultery is widely practised but publicly condemned. The American cultural ideal, which bears no relationship of any sort to American cultural reality, is a monogamous marriage between two virgins. In America, one should never admit to adultery, much less having enjoyed it. Political figures in particular are held to very strict standards of marital fidelity, in spite of the fact that they are among the least likely to observe such conventions. Cries of outrage are heard when an affair is discovered and it is universally assumed that the spouses will immediately divorce. But the most vicious scorn of all is directed at couples who choose to stay married: "How can she/he stay with him/her after what he/she did?"

All this sex doesn't mean Americans feel that they know what they're doing. Contraceptives, once relegated to the back of the counter at pharmacies, are now sold everywhere from petrol stations to newsstands, but conservative parents have long opposed school-based public sex education programmes on religious grounds. As a result, many Americans are surprisingly ignorant of the basic mechanics of reproduction. This is a main reason for America's high teenage pregnancy rate.

Sex is a particularly touchy subject at work, where even a hint of sexual harassment can bring on a damaging lawsuit. Garage mechanics can no longer post calendars with photographs of nude women, and supervisors who tell racy jokes to their secretaries are endangering their careers. However, Americans are finally getting around to admitting that attitudes towards sex differ between men and women, and researchers have recently traced this disparity to biology. Thus, a wandering husband can now offer the defence, "I can't help it, honey. It's genetic."

Manners

Americans are intrigued by good manners, in part because they don't have any. In the past few years middle-class parents have realised that their children not only don't know which fork to use at a formal dinner but rarely use a fork at all. It seems beside the point that this is due in large part to the fact that said children are eating most of their meals at fast-food restaurants with their friends instead of around the family table.

Manners are back, up to a point, and etiquette schools do a brisk trade in educating young savages in the niceties of proper behaviour, American-style. However, manners have had to adapt to a number of situations hitherto unthought of. How does one introduce one's son and his live-in male companion? What role does the stepfather of the bride play in the wedding ceremony? Should a woman introduce her children to her new boyfriend on the first date?

Americans manage to combine an overall public rudeness with heartfelt concern for others' welfare. They talk too loudly, chew with their mouths open, cut each other off at intersections when driving, and take the last doughnut without a second thought. Yet they are generous to charities, kind to animals, and concerned about the welfare of the poor.

Many of the variations in American public behaviour are regional. Urban New Yorkers are chatty but brusque, giving them the reputation for being intrusive and rude, whereas the friendly Midwesterners can take so long to get to the point that it takes a half an hour to buy a bar of soap.

Smoking

Americans mind if you smoke, they mind very much, and not being a shy race, they will frequently let you know just exactly how much they mind. In certain areas of the United States, being a smoker is not only personal but social suicide.

Smoking is now something of a class indicator, separating the workers from the management. A country honky-tonk bar reeks of tobacco, but in the Ritz-Carlton lounge it's a sure bet that any smokers will be German or Japanese tourists or tobacco company executives planning how to diversify their holdings.

I'm Late, I'm Late!

Like Alice's White Rabbit, Americans (particularly big-city Americans) run around in a frenzy of worry over what time it is. This doesn't mean they are prompt; far from it. Americans tend to run late, particularly if they're important or wealthy. Powerful Americans guard their time jealously and charge handsomely for it. Lawyers bill their clients in six-minute increments and if an executive earning $80 million a year spends two or three minutes on pleasantries, he's tossing thousands out the window and knows it.

Sense of Humour

Americans have a strong taste for slapstick in various forms, and substitute riposte and banter for irony or whimsy, which they tend not to understand.

Because everyone has ancestors, family and friends of every possible race, colour, creed and national origin, and because sensitivity to such differences has reached unprecedented tenderness in recent years, it is considered rude to tell a joke that perpetuates an ethnic, social, religious, sexual, or racial stereotype. Pat and Mike, Rastus and Festus, the drunk priest, the Polish bridegroom, the silly blonde – all are now off-limits, at least in public. That still leaves plenty of material for humour, such as occupation, political persuasion, or region of origin. For example, a Texan was boasting to an Arkansan about his ranch. "Why, my ranch is so big," he said, "that if I start out in my truck in the morning to drive around it, it's night by the time I get home." The Arkansan nodded understandingly and said, "Yep. I had a truck like that once."

The only group detested enough to be a suitable butt for barbed humour is lawyers. Lawyers are unpopular because they're only consulted in times of distress, such as during divorces, negligence suits and second-degree murder defences. Any lawyer joke is sure to draw a laugh. Some lawyer jokes are specific:

Q: Why don't sharks bite lawyers?
A: Professional courtesy.

Q: Why does Arizona have lots of vultures and Washington, DC have lots of lawyers?
A: Arizona got first choice.

Did you hear that medical laboratories have started using lawyers instead of white rats? There are more of them, researchers don't get as attached to them, and there are some things even a laboratory rat just won't do.

Others are merely old ethnic jokes adapted to the needs of the target:

Q: What do you have when you have two lawyers buried up to their necks in sand?
A: Not enough sand.

Politicians are also fair game, but since approximately two-thirds of the nation's congressional representatives are law school graduates, such jokes are really just a subset of the 'lawyer' canon.

Perhaps the most characteristic expression of American humour is the snappy retort. A classic example comes from comedian Jack Benny, famous for his parsimony. A criminal pointed a gun at Benny and said, "Your money or your life." Benny hesitated a few moments and answered, "I'm thinking, I'm thinking."

Obsessions

The American Image

There are a few, a very few things that Americans condemn as being beyond the pale. They include growing old, being fat and dying.

Growing Old

There is nothing more antithetical to the American ideal than growing old. The cultural message for both men and women is 'Look 20 years younger'. Old people, who are called seniors, fight the man with the scythe by dyeing their hair, wearing blue jeans, and having their faces lifted and their tummies tucked. Perhaps the definitive American remark on aging was made by Ivana Trump, who said, "I'll always look 35, but it's going to cost Donald a lot of money." (It didn't work. He dumped her for a younger woman, but she got the kids and the Plaza Hotel.)

Being Fat

An American socialite once said: "You can never be too rich or too thin." All Americans crave to be svelte (and rich). This doesn't mean the average person is thin; far from it. At any given moment fully 30% of all women are on a weight-loss diet and another 50% are clinically obese. However, rich women are thinner than the non-rich, as perusal of any society page will show.

Fat is one of the great American paradoxes: films, television, and magazines all idolise undernourished fashion waifs; the weight-loss industry generates billions of dollars per year, yet back in the heartland Mr and Mrs America are dolloping extra mayonnaise on their Big Macs and tucking into a large order of fries. Ironically, discrimination against fat people is tolerated in a way that would be unthinkable for any other form of prejudice.

Dying

It's in extremely bad taste for an American to die, not to mention inconsiderate to loved ones and friends. Americans try to pretend that death doesn't happen at all, and certainly not to their own personal selves. When someone does die, Americans don't know what to say and try to put the experience behind them as soon as possible. Mentioning death in polite society is considered morbid unless it's in the context of a lurid murder.

Getting sick is in almost as bad taste as dying (and significantly more expensive). When an American asks "How are you?" he or she knows the answer already: "Fine, thanks. And you?"

Gadgets

Do you need to chop lettuce? Dry your hair? Buff your fingernails? Cook a hot dog? Make popcorn? Scent the air? If so, America has an electrical appliance constructed specifically for that purpose, and it can be acquired either from a drugstore or by calling the telephone number of an advertisement on late-night television.

American inventiveness, not satisfied with giving the world the automobile, the airplane, colour television, cellular telephone and the Internet, has tackled less obvious needs. Americans own thousands of specialised tools that address nearly every human requirement, however obscure. This is the land of the electric salad dryer, the electric can opener, the electric soap dispenser, the electric air freshener, the electric hair curler, the in-the-shell egg scrambler and the electric tweezers. Heaven forbid one should have to do anything manually.

Right now American brides by the thousands are opening boxes containing electric bread-baking machines and pasta makers. Meanwhile, their parents' electric carving knives, electric woks and electric casserole warmers gather dust.

Leisure and Pleasure

If there's one thing at which the United States excels, it is amusing itself and the world. Not that Americans have much time for leisure. As most workers receive only two weeks of paid leave each year, the mini-vacation is very popular. People head out of town for a long weekend of three or four days so as not to burn up all their holiday time at once.

The United States offers vast holiday resources. The average family *modus operandi* for holidays is to pack the children and a huge amount of luggage into a car or RV (recreational vehicle – a motorised small house with all the comforts of home) and drive thousands of miles. Favourite activities include camping, fishing, and visiting America's national monuments and sights. The fact that all these attractions are separated by hundreds of miles of Interstate only adds to the fun.

When they go on holiday Americans become even more American than usual, if that's possible, wearing crazy-patterned shorts, white running shoes, and T-shirts with offensive slogans. They carry their wallets in crescent-shaped 'fanny packs' that only emphasise their girth, and patronise ice cream and fudge vendors. Americans at home despise holiday-makers who clog the streets and eat too much. Then on their own two weeks off they'll dress up, get in the Winnebago (a popular RV), and go and do it all themselves.

Sport

A polyglot, varied country like the United States needs a national lingua franca, something that allows the members of any minority subculture to communicate on a friendly basis with people from vastly different backgrounds. Sport is this language. Formerly restricted largely to males, sports talk has become the universal means of communication as the genders approach social equality.

A legal change in 1972 opened the way to women's participation in college sports. Women now have their own basketball league and the women's soccer team is a world champion. Ask the average American to name a famous soccer player, the answer might be Mia Hamm or Brandi Chastain, not one of those loser guys.

Major cities have a professional football, baseball, basketball, or hockey team, while smaller towns make do with a high school, college, or minor league team. The sports year may be divided roughly into baseball in summer, football in autumn, basketball in spring, and hockey forever. In practice, the seasons overlap – a hectic scheduling which prevents the television from ever becoming completely idle and gives American males a year-round excuse to escape weekend chores.

Every American football and basketball team, from high school on up to the professional leagues, has an auxiliary squad of attractive young women who wave pom-poms and lead the fans in various cheers. Just as every American boy yearns to be a football quarterback, so girls yearn to head the cheerleading squad, amidst vicious real-life rivalry.

Seats for professional sporting events are neither cheap nor, in some cases, easy to get. In Washington, DC, for example, the waiting list for season football tickets is several decades long. The good news for sports fans is on cable television, where various all-sports channels broadcast every conceivable game. New split-screen technology allows addicts to watch several games at once.

The Big Game

There are big games, and then there is The Big Game – the Superbowl. The Superbowl is the most important event in the world, probably in the universe. A lot of sports fans would argue that this annual American football game is the most important event of any kind ever held, certainly more important than the invasion of Normandy or the inauguration of a new president.

This end-of-January extravaganza purports to be the World Championship of a game that is only played professionally in North America. (There is a World League of American Football, but the chances of one of its teams playing in the Superbowl any time soon are thinner than a cheerleader's panties.)

The game's promoters select a stadium that's as large as possible in a city that's warm enough so that wealthy fans won't freeze to death, usually somewhere in Florida, California, or Texas. For maximum dollar impact, the game is scheduled to allow easy viewing in all the main American time zones, and advertisers trot out their most innovative commercials for the Superbowl, paying upwards of $2,200,000 a minute for the privilege of showing them. This may well be worth it, since on Superbowl Sunday more than half of all American televisions are tuned to The Game.

On Superbowl Sunday, Americans hold parties to watch television and consume beer, pizza and nachos. In a city that has a team playing in the Superbowl, all public activity stops and traffic disappears. When the game is over, riotous celebrations, or sometimes just riots, break out in the neighbourhood with the most bars.

Born to Shop

The American love affair with shopping is more than the natural by-product of a materialistic society. Shopping isn't a chore, it's recreation. It's a pleasure, an amusement, a way to spend time. Friends will make a date to go shopping together and happily return home empty-handed.

The most popular tourist attraction in the state of Virginia is not Mount Vernon, home of president George Washington, nor Monticello, home of president Thomas Jefferson, nor even Williamsburg, the colonial capital-cum-theme park originally restored by the Rockefellers. It's Potomac Mills, a shopping centre about 20 miles south of Washington, DC.

American shopping malls (and supermarkets) are palaces of consumerism, vast labyrinths of shops and restaurants. Surrounded by many acres of car parks, laden with costly merchandise from all over the world, America's malls beckon with glitter and lights. In suburban communities (now called 'edge cities'), it's common for schools to hold dances and parties in shopping malls. They're clean and safe and patrolled by private security guards who have far broader latitude than publicly funded police.

The ultimate in shopping convenience, of course, is the Internet, now rapidly replacing mail-order. At one time Sears Roebuck even sold houses by mail-order. Many are sturdy and habitable 90 years on. Today, every home still receives hundreds of coloured catalogues offering every imaginable item (and some unimaginable items) through the mail. But the interactive Internet is faster and more fun to use than old-fashioned, low-tech paper. Armed with a computer and a credit card, an American can, and will, outfit a household without budging an inch.

Even grocery shopping has gone electronic – Americans can click on a picture of frozen peas and have the real thing show up the next day in an insulated wrapper. Some Americans go on line for everything, such as making investments, learning to drive, or finding someone to marry.

Attitudes and Values

Money

As writer and social critic Fran Lebowitz puts it, "In this country, they don't only think time is money. They think everything is money." On consideration, the truth is obvious: in the United States, everything really is money. In an egalitarian society of self-made men, what use is a noble family? What good is a developed spiritual nature in the hard-battling arena of technology and commerce? How valuable are clean hands and a pure heart when it's a dog-eat-dog world? Americans think of everything in terms of money because money can be quantified. In the game of life, money is the most effective way to keep score.

The goal of the Founding Fathers was to create a society

without hereditary distinctions; George Washington turned down the offer of a kingship and chose the presidency instead. Unfortunately, egalitarianism left a tremendous snobbery gap, since nobody could feel better than anybody else simply by reason of birth. Money is the great de-equalizer.

Americans are quite open about their obsession with money. They cheerfully ask and tell each other what possessions cost and how much they earn (though the latter figure is often inflated for public consumption), and have conversations like, "How much did your lawyer charge you for your divorce? Really? Wow. I guess I got a better deal than I thought."

Class and Social Status

Almost every American, when asked, will describe him or herself as middle class. (For practical purposes, middle class means having a job.) Today's Americans no longer believe that anyone can grow up to be president, and are only too conscious of the vast gaps in welfare between their richest and poorest citizens. But they haven't given up all illusions of equality.

America provides vast social mobility. A plumber could easily have a son who's a college professor, and just as easily, a college professor could have a son who's a plumber, especially when the son discovers the direction of the salary differential between the two professions.

In other countries those with hereditary wealth may lead lives of ostentatious indolence. In the United States even those who don't need to work pretend they do. Anyone without a job is a non-person. An American conversational staple is to ask, "What do you do?" (often followed by "Where are you from?"). The only forbidden answer is "Nothing. I'm rich."

When they talk about class, Americans mean a loose consideration of background and attitude that is unrelated to wealth. Donald Trump, for example, while possessed of great wealth, has remarkably little class, while Katherine Hepburn has class down to her toes.

Immigrants

Every new wave of immigrants is met with hostility by the old. The Dutch in Nieuw Amsterdam (now New York) viewed the English arrivistes with suspicion; the English mistrusted the Germans, who refused to hire the Irish, who discriminated against the Russians and Poles, who won't live next to the Vietnamese, and so on. Nobody already in the United States wants to let anybody new enter.

Like it or not, Mexico sends hundreds of thousands of its citizens north across its (heavily patrolled and fenced) border every year. Through sheer population pressure Mexico is accomplishing what no other foreign government has ever seriously attempted: conquest of the United States. In the American west and southwest, Spanish is the unofficial second language and signs and government documents provide information in Spanish as a matter of course. Office workers who want the rubbish taken out write 'BASURA' instead of 'TRASH' on the boxes.

An American's Car is His Castle

The automobile, along with a house and a garden, is an essential element of the American Dream.

The average American household has 1.7 vehicles (210 million vehicles in a country of 275 million people); each vehicle is driven an average of 12,000 miles per year at an average highway speed of 59 miles per hour, though some Interstates are so congested that rush-hour speeds may be less than half that. (An average of 75% of vehicles ignore the posted 65-mile-per-hour legal speed limit: those that don't have just seen a police car.) Most cars are used for daily commuting; less than 6% of the American workforce uses public transportation to get to work. Some of the country's wonderful high-speed highways now carry three or more times the intended amount of traffic and twice a day turn into parking lots. Los Angeles and Washington, DC, win the prize for the two cities with the worst congestion.

Even if suburban residents could walk to anything other than the house next door, they wouldn't. Walking is un-American. Whenever possible, Americans drive and, if necessary, wait to get a parking place close to their destination. Congestion occurs as drivers circle the shops, looking for a parking space that's closer to where they want to go.

American cars are all air-conditioned and automatic. A 'stick shift' (manual) is harder to drive and therefore considered sportier, more masculine. (Continually pressing on the clutch can get tiresome if one drives 30 miles each way to work in heavy traffic, as many Americans do.) An American man might buy a non-automatic so his wife won't be able to drive it – and vice versa.

A car is not just an American's castle, it's a suit of clothes, a haircut, a display of one's personality to the world. Car owners not only select vehicles that reflect this, from red Mazda Miatas to long black Mercedes, they also customise them in innumerable ways. They paint the cars with flames, stripes, or woodland scenes; they add mirrors and chrome and special headlights; they put shingles all over old schoolbuses and turn them into holiday motor homes. (Japanese cars are disparagingly referred to as 'rice rockets' or 'econoboxes'. Small

European cars are not permitted on the road at all because they are a hazard on the highways.)

More conventional drivers satisfy themselves with bumper stickers that reveal their educational background, political opinions, or marital status, from 'Yale School of Law' to 'If you're rich, I'm single'.

But the biggest purveyors of automotive messages are state governments, which offer special licence plates for a few extra dollars. These 'vanity tags' allow drivers to identify their vehicles with six or seven numbers and letters they choose themselves. This has spawned an elaborate form of coded communication, with car owners outdoing each other to see who is the cleverest. A snappy red convertible might have 6UL DV8. A dentist might have 2TH DR or MOLAR, while a Tonkinese cat fancier has TONK MOM and a lawyer TORTS. A patriotic Chevy pickup advises H8 4N TRX, while sedate black sedans with Clergy medallions offer INRI or III XVI, an allusion to the verse from the Gospel of St John. Political opinions abound, e.g. DEM CAR and LEFANT.

Applications are checked for potential obscenity, but with mixed success; most state employees are not multi-lingual. A citizen requesting GOV SUX was turned down, protested publicly, and got his tag.*

Church versus State

America has no official religion of any sort, other than the near-universal worship of Mammon and widespread devotion to the cult of Disney. The Constitution forbids establishment of religion and effectively separates all

---

*For the rebus-impaired, the above tags include 'sexual deviate', 'tooth doctor', 'hate foreign trucks', 'Democrat car', 'elephant', a symbol of the Republican party, and 'Government sucks'.

political and religious activity. Spoken prayer is forbidden at school graduations, and towns may not use public funds to display nativity scenes at Christmas.

Americans are entitled to attend the church of their choice. Freedom of religion even extends to inventing one's own. Anyone who wants to can start a religion. Indeed, religion can be a profitable enterprise, since religious institutions do not pay taxes and contributions to them are tax-deductible. Such new churches have names like the Church Universal and Triumphant, the Universal Life Church, and the Bible Rock Church of God. However, the most influential American-born religion is the Church of the Latter-Day Saints in Utah, also known as the Mormons, which has millions of members around the world and continues to grow.

In the area known as the Bible Belt, an ill-defined zone that stretches roughly from the lower East Coast westward towards Missouri and Kansas, small independent churches sprout like cotton plants, usually preaching variations on the popular themes that evolution is a lie, unbelievers are going to hell, and God likes America best.

Americans like to believe that the world cannot possibly function without their presence. Thus, periodically someone will predict the end of the world, usually based on a new mathematical interpretation of the book of Revelations or observation of an astronomical anomaly. Occasionally the hysteria becomes fairly widespread as thousands of people turn into True Believers in order to reserve a good seat for the Ultimate Superbowl. The fact that they are invariably disappointed doesn't stop them from doing it all again at a later date.

Custom and Tradition

Holidays

As a secular country, the United States has trouble with holidays because religious observances and saint's days are off-limits as far as the public calendar is concerned. Yet the traditional cultural observances are mainly religious in nature. What's a non-sectarian nation to do?

To solve the problem, the Americans observe their holidays on a two-tier system. In the first tier are the official government holidays, primarily patriotic, which comprise a dozen or so days commemorating notable men and important civil events. Most of these float to the nearest Monday to provide a series of three-day weekends for office drones. Banks and workplaces are closed, there is no mail delivery, and public institutions in general shut down. Shops are open, however. In America, the shops are always open, except on Christmas Day.

Observance of most secular holidays is limited to parades, speeches, and enthusiastically advertised department store sales. But in the American ritual calendar, the three summer holidays – Memorial Day, the Fourth of July (Independence Day), and Labour Day – are consecrated to outdoor barbecues. All across the country homeowners dust off their Weber grills, open packs of hot dogs for the children and trays of chicken, steak, or ribs for the adults, douse lumps of charcoal in evil-smelling flammable liquids, and proceed to carbonise the meat, pollute the air, and irritate their stomachs. Holding backyard barbecues is popular all summer long, of course, but on those three days it's mandatory.

The Fourth of July domestic culinary pyromania is followed by community pyrotechnics. Every town puts on the most lavish public fireworks display it can afford, and many families light their own Roman candles and sparklers. Since fireworks laws vary from state to state, a certain amount of smuggling goes on, with interesting fireworks flowing from states with the laxest controls to states that place more emphasis on public safety.

The population at large also observes a dozen or more unofficial holidays, which celebrate various aspects of religion and popular culture, and which are promoted by the retail, greeting card, and floral industries – such as National Secretary's Day, Grandparents' Day, and Sweetest Day, which was initiated by the employee of a candy company in Chicago in the 1930s to distribute candy and gifts to city's orphans, along with the sick and shut-in, and so called because the gestures were the sort that elicited a cry of "That's so sweet!"

St Patrick's Day turns everybody in the United States into honorary Irishmen and women. Everything turns green, even things not normally seen in that colour. Bars serve green beer, bakeries produce green bagels, Chicago goes the extra mile and dyes the river green.

It is traditional on St Patrick's day to consume a minimum of one serving of an alcoholic beverage in an Irish bar, and on this day all bars become Irish, as do all musicians. The nation's real alcoholics refer to St Patrick's Day as 'amateur night'.

Few holidays tap into the American psyche so closely as Halloween*. Some of the nation's most distinctive character traits – exhibitionism, religious extremism, paranoia, and greed – all come together on Halloween to celebrate, protest, and turn a profit. Adults and children alike wear costumes, often to work (air travellers may find their flight attendants dressed as witches or fairies). Religiously conservative parents make annual attempts to ban Halloween pumpkins and ghost costumes from schools because, they claim, it teaches the children to

* which is now the second most expensive, after Christmas.

worship Satan. Other parents allow their children to go trick-or-treating (code for 'give me some candy or I'll drape toilet paper all over your shrubbery') – but then, fearing sabotage, take the candy to the airport or police station so it can be X-rayed for foreign objects. (The 'razor blade in the apple' story is a hardy perennial.)

New Year's Eve features humiliation of a qualitatively different sort: if one is single, it becomes essential to find a companion for this, the most important date night of the year. Being dateless on New Year's Eve is proof positive of a person's social and sexual undesirability.

Celebrations on the East Coast centre around televised events from Times Square, New York, the official arbiter of just when the New Year arrives. But since the United States covers five time zones, the New Year hops across the country in one-hour jumps, and by the time Hawaii blows its noisemakers for the New Year, the rest of the country is fast asleep.

Family Gatherings

Thanksgiving, the third Thursday in November, is time for far-flung families to join around a common table. Grown children brave the busiest travel season of the year to return to their ancestral nest, where they eat too much, drink too much, and pick up year-old arguments as though they had never left home.

The traditional meal centres around a roast turkey stuffed with breadcrumbs and sage, supplemented by a generous assortment of candied yams topped with baby marshmallows, mashed potatoes with gravy, baked potatoes, potatoes au gratin, baked winter squash, mashed winter squash, jellied salad, green salad, stewed tomatoes, canned green beans, creamed onions, brussels sprouts, cornbread, dinner rolls, cranberry relish, celery, olives, pumpkin pie, apple pie, mince pie, Indian pudding, and ice cream. The goal is to eat so much that nobody can move, and then watch football on television. On this day it is traditional to bow one's head and give thanks for life's many blessings. However, most celebrants are actually silently giving thanks that they only see their families once a year.

Showers

In America any change of status – birthdays, anniversaries, leaving a job, getting married, having a baby – warrants a celebration of some sort. New brides and the newly pregnant are treated to a 'shower', at which guests (traditionally all female) shower the bride or mother-to-be with gifts. Depending on the occasion, offerings range from the utilitarian (towels, an electric frying pan) to the salacious (massage oil and crotchless panties).

Bigger and Better

Americans give the merest mumbling lip service to the metric system, while continuing to quantify almost everything with the tried-and-true units of measurement they have used since before the French Revolution.

Certain measures, however, are more important than others and are based on units that may not be found in any standard conversion table. Some standard United States units of measure include the following:

The toaster oven. In the late 20th century the toaster oven replaced the breadbox both as a domestic appliance and as a standard unit of volume, often for humorous references. ("We were attacked by mosquitoes the size of toaster ovens.")

The football field. A regulation American football field is 100 yards long and 160 feet wide (91 x 48 metres). Any large flat area, such as the deck of an aircraft carrier, the amount of paper used to print the *San Francisco Examiner*, or the exterior of the World Trade Center, is described as being "as big as *n* football fields".

The New York minute. Everything moves faster in New York City, including time. A New York minute is thus much shorter than sixty seconds, indeed, it's almost instantaneous: "I'd go out with Sandra Bullock in a New York minute."

The wind-chill factor. Not satisfied by measuring ambient temperature with an obsolete system, Americans invented the wind-chill factor, which combines degrees Fahrenheit with air velocity to create a number that's much more impressive. For example, when a temperature of 32°F combines with a 10-mile-an-hour wind, the wind-chill factor drops to 20°F, which sounds a lot colder and makes those who venture out in it feel hardy and adventurous. In summer what is called the 'comfort index' takes over, combining temperature with humidity to prove that getting the central air-conditioning replaced last year really was worth the money.

Currency. American coins and bills have been specifically designed to confuse natives of other nations. Coins include the penny, nickel, dime, and quarter, not one of which is labelled with its actual cents' value in numerals. American folding money is green, of uniform size and design, with a picture of a dead president on it. Thus a $10 bill (or note) looks a lot like a $1 bill or a $100 bill. Since the largest bill in general circulation is $20 (a deliberate move to make large cash transactions obvious and cumbersome and thus discourage crime), the confusion doesn't affect the average American, who never pays cash anyway and uses a credit card for all purchases costlier than a Coke.

Good Looks and Hygiene

Frenchmen worry about their livers. Germans worry about their excretory abilities. Americans worry about their hair. The hair on their heads, that is. Women remove most of their other hair, including the bits that stick out around what is charmingly euphemised as 'the bikini line'.

When asked in a survey what they notice first in a potential mate, the answer from both men and women was hair. Having good hair is more important than having a college education or a happy family.

American drug stores burst with hair care products: shampoos, conditioners, cream rinses, spray-on detanglers, permanent colourants, temporary colourants, setting gels, styling mousses, gloss enhancers, curl relaxers, curl activators and holding sprays. This means that the average American's hair contains more chemicals than Bhopal. Every American woman has at least one hair dryer, and usually a curling iron and electric rollers besides, not to mention styling brushes, smoothing brushes, holding combs, barrettes, clips, bands and other decorations. Men also have hair dryers and, if they suffer from baldness, they use a growth stimulator, buy hairpieces, or have hair transplanted from the hirsute part of the scalp to the bare areas.

Hair makes a political as well as a personal statement. In the 1960s, an Afro hairstyle was a badge of independence among African Americans. Recruits into the US Marines have their heads shaved as part of their introduction to military life and are called 'jarheads' as a result, though not to their faces. The 'big hair' look is a badge of femininity and often denotes social class as well. The worst personal crisis an American can endure is a 'bad hair day'.

Hillary Clinton was famous for changing her hairstyle as First Lady; when she became a Senator she changed it yet again. Clinton himself made headline news when he had his hair cut, allegedly for $400, in his airplane on the runway of Los Angeles airport. The mockery this provoked rings hollow, though. Every American would love to get a $400 haircut.

Body Hair and Odour

Excess body hair is taboo, especially in females. American women shave their legs and armpits and assume that any hairy-legged woman is a lesbian out to destroy the American Way of Life.

The odour of the human body is considered repulsive. Americans like pleasant scents, and douse themselves and their personal products liberally with perfume. They use deodorant in their armpits (which they delicately call 'underarms'), spray their homes with room freshener, put fuzzy dice with air freshener in their cars and drape their bathrooms with scented toilet tissue.

In the Bathroom Cupboard

Anyone with something to hide wouldn't keep it in the medicine cabinet. Visitors have a habit of opening the door just to have a peek while washing their hands. One ingenious hostess punishes prying dinner guests by filling her medicine cabinet with marbles, which fall noisily into the washbasin when the door is opened.

What they are likely to find is:

- Deodorant, because Americans not only sweat more than Europeans (it's hot in America), they worry more about the odour.
- Antacids, because indigestion is part of the American way of life (and diet).

- Allergy, sinus and headache medication, especially during the various pollen seasons.
- Tranquillisers or anti-depressants, to alleviate the stress of being American.

Heartache

The heart is amazing – it beats more than 30 million times a year, pumping life-giving oxygen throughout the body, without getting tired or ever taking a day off. It's a very American kind of muscle.

Americans don't take their hearts for granted. Heart disease is a leading killer, and there isn't a sentient American who doesn't know this on some level. Americans fear cancer with a deadly terror, but they fear a heart attack even more. Health-minded Americans shun activities linked with heart disease, such as smoking and eating fatty foods, and engage religiously in vigorous exercise, known as 'working out'. Joggers can be seen on the streets in droves soon after dawn, and health clubs and gyms dot the landscape of major cities. In an exercise in irony, most health club members drive to an exercise studio to go running on a treadmill.

Heart fear is largely, although not exclusively, a masculine phenomenon. "You'll give me a heart attack!" an American father screams at his teenage daughter as she leaves the house wearing a couple of handkerchiefs and a bit of gold string. The daughter usually reacts by bringing home a series of unsuitable males to see if Daddy will put his money where his mouth is. Some fathers make good on their promise, some don't.

For some men fear of a heart attack is an incentive to fidelity. Every once in a while a famous public figure suffers a heart attack while alone in the company of a person who is not his wife. The resulting publicity does wonders for the nation's marriages.

Not everyone in the country has stopped smoking and drinking and eating steak or started exercising, of course, but they know they should. Evidence that a glass of red wine every day helps prevent heart attacks gives these people much hope.

Health Care and Doctors

One reason Americans are obsessed with staying healthy is that it is much, much cheaper than getting sick. American medical care, like so much else in the United States, is the finest that money can buy, but then one needs money to buy it. The system that provides medical services includes a bewildering array of public and private facilities reimbursed by a patchwork of privately funded and government-mandated insurance schemes that usually cover part, but not all, of the cost of treatment. For non-emergencies, proof of insurance is a prerequisite for receiving care in a private hospital. Even an insured person who becomes ill may be presented with a bill for 20% or more of the (significant) treatment cost. The end result is that for many Americans a bout of illness is also the broad road to bankruptcy.

Part of the ruinous expense comes from the potential for lawsuits. A doctor who delivers a defective baby, for example, may end up personally liable for millions of dollars to pay for that child's lifelong care. Enter the spectre of malpractice insurance, which can add as much as $500 to the cost of every hospital delivery.

The medical question 'Who's your insurance company?' sets into motion a maelstrom of paperwork and forms, often requiring months and many telephone calls to unravel. A patient who cannot pay is turned over to a collection agency, like any other deadbeat.

Americans treat doctors with a strange mixture of awe, respect, cynicism, and contempt. A number of jokes reflect their unique perspective – e.g. St Peter was welcoming a new arrival when a red Ferrari driven by a bearded older man in a tweed hat zoomed at full speed through the pearly gates. 'Who's that?' asked the new arrival. 'Oh,' said St Peter, 'That's God. He thinks he's a doctor.'

Culture

Though the fine arts do exist in the United States, often heavily subsidised by government and charitable foundations, the country's true pulse is popular. Ever the beacon of democracy, America produces culture of the people, by the people, and for the people, all the people, all over the world.

American popular culture is, in fact, the most popular pop culture ever invented. A dubbed version of *The X-Files* blares from televisions in Brazil and China, Spanish señoritas munch McDonald's in Madrid, and Thai taxis travel to the rhythms of Madonna.

Like King Canute, foreign governments occasionally try to stop the rising tide of American cultural influence, and like the hapless king they always fail. The tsunami that is American popular culture sweeps aside everything in its path.

Television

Television is the single strongest cultural influence on American life and the widely recognised lowest common denominator. More homes have televisions than indoor plumbing, and the average child spends more time watching television than he or she does in the classroom.

Television defines a reality of its own; news that isn't covered on television didn't happen, and television-only events (such as the wedding or the death of a fictitious character) provoke nationwide reactions.

Daytime shows lean towards endless soap operas with plots that revolve around infidelity and medical crises, and talk shows in which hosts prod their guests to reveal personal details no sane person would want to make public.

The American passion for getting something for nothing reaches a frenzy in evening game shows. Another evening staple is the hard-boiled investigative show, which dwells on lurid topics such as body-snatching, drug dealing, and juvenile male prostitution. The latest development in this genre is the real-life crime show, on which cameramen follow the police around for an evening and film them making arrests.

Every time you think that no depth is unplumbed, sure enough, television finds a format even more degrading. *Survivor*, for example, pits a dozen castaways against each other in meaningless competitions; the individual who can endure the most humiliation gets a million dollars. In *Temptation Island* a number of supposedly happy couples are marooned on an island with a variety of sexy singletons who try to break them up.

Television reached its acme, or perhaps more accurately its nadir, with the introduction of cable and satellite TV, which provides hundreds of channels of unwatchable drivel. Specialised programmes include The Weather Channel, 24 hours a day of barometry and precipitation forecasts; Music Television (MTV) and its country music and soul music imitators; C-Span, which shows the US Congress in session and is widely applied as a soporific; and Court TV, which allows viewers to shriek at the television judge the way sports fans might shriek at a referee.

Few topics are considered cultural minefields. Turn on an American television any afternoon and you can see people discussing, in intimate detail, before millions of viewers, topics that natives of other nations wouldn't whisper about in the dark. One may hear the testimony of a man who had a sex-change operation so he could live a fulfilled life as a lesbian, or a wife who had a baby by her sister's husband and wants another so the child will have siblings (her own husband doesn't know about the situation, but presumably will soon if he's at home watching television). Talk-show guests include everything from homosexual fathers to bisexual nuns to children who killed their parents, interspersed with advertisements for laxatives.

Faced with such unabashed exhibitionism, one is tempted to scream, "Is nothing sacred?" The answer, of course, is "Well, actually, no. Not on television, anyway."

Eating and Drinking

You Are What You Eat

Americans approach every meal in terror that the food will leap up off their plate and kill them or, worse, make them fat. Diet contributes to disease, particularly heart disease, and one never knows which mouthful could be fatal. Suspicious dishes include steak (a 'heart attack on a plate') and any high-fat, high-cholesterol, high-calorie, low-fibre food, such as sugar, butter, cheese, ice cream, white bread, or fried anything. Hot dogs, an American staple, have been linked with leukemia in children. Even spinach and beets are not exempt, since they are high in oxalic acid, which is harmful in large quantities. In the endless American battle for eternal youth, glowing good health and an attractive figure, food is on the front lines, and flavour is the first casualty.

The American dietary obsession is fed by a seemingly endless series of scientific studies that demonstrate the wholesomeness or toxicity of various foodstuffs. When one study found that eating massive quantities of oat bran reduced cholesterol and thus might help prevent heart attacks, the price of oats skyrocketed and American supermarkets were instantly flooded with products containing oat bran, including oat bran candy bars and oat bran beer.

Americans will eat any disgusting and tasteless substance, especially if they can be convinced it will keep them healthy or make them thin. Restaurants put special symbols on their menus to indicate dishes that are 'heart healthy' (low in cholesterol and saturated fat) or 'light' (an indefinite term that implies, but does not necessarily mean, low calorie or low fat). Supermarkets have aisles of items marked 'low salt', 'low calorie', 'low fat', 'diet', 'cholesterol-free' or 'imitation'. (The label 'low flavour' would be superfluous.) Americans buy uniform strips of 'bacon' extruded from soyabeans, liquid fake eggs in little plastic cartons, fat-free cheese that resembles recycled running shoes, carbonated sodas flavoured with chemicals they can't even pronounce, and high-fibre bread bulked out with wood pulp.

The food itself isn't nearly as repellent as the food bore. A food bore will preach about the benefits of whatever regimen he or she is following, and (especially in California) is only too willing to explain just how a particular diet is beneficial. Any discussion is larded with comments like "Eating more vegetables prevents cancer, you know", or "It isn't fat that makes you fat, it's carbohydrates that make you fat", or "Do you *know* how veal is raised?"

Forbidden foods, particularly chocolate, arouse the same illicit thrill in Americans that other cultures reserve for sex. American diners feel a delicious quiver of guilt with every mouthful of chocolate mousse or Boston cream pie. Rich, 'sinful' desserts have sinister names like Devil's Food Cake, Chocolate Madness, or Death By Chocolate. They're just explaining what every American already knows: eating may be hazardous to your health.

The American Breakfast

Breakfast has an honoured place in the American diet. Restaurants post signs advertising 'Breakfast served until 11 a.m.' or, in the case of all-night diners, 'Breakfast 24 hours a day'.

Breakfast food, which can be highly regional, includes cold cereal with milk, bacon, coffee, oatmeal, sausage, ham, eggs, scrapple (made from the parts of the pig unfit for sausage), coffee, biscuits (like English scones), home-fried potatoes, toast, fried corn meal mush, maple syrup, coffee, waffles, corned beef hash, pancakes, coffee and grits.

Grits are a quintessentially American dish. They are made from maize that has been soaked in water and treated with caustic lye to scientifically remove every vestige of colour and flavour. Grits look like white, lumpy oatmeal and have less taste than wallpaper paste unless and until they are liberally doused with butter, salt and gravy (especially red-eye gravy, which is made with pan drippings and coffee). Southerners adore them. Northerners think they're the reason the South lost the Civil War. Starting somewhere around Maryland an invisible line crosses the country: below it grits are considered essential for life, while above it they're banned as being unfit for human consumption.

Restaurants

American restaurants range from informal, where the counter attendant says "Hi, what'll you have?", to formal, where the waiter says "Hello, I'm Alan and I'll be your server for this evening. Shall I tell you about tonight's specials?" On occasion the waiter or waitress may even sit down and chat for a few moments to discuss the intricacies of the menu. Intrusive service is what Americans prefer. Some restaurants are famous for the surliness of their waiters and waitresses, using bad manners to attract masochistic munchers by the roomful.

The most typical American restaurants offer no service at all. In 1954, Ray Kroc bought the rights to the McDonald brothers' hamburger stand and began selling franchises. There are now more than 28,000 McDonald's worldwide selling hundreds of millions of hamburgers a year. The McDonald's recipe for success involves serving a very limited menu of popular foods, mainly hamburgers, French fries, and milkshakes, minimising labour costs by breaking preparation down into quantified routine tasks, using disposable packages to eliminate the cost of dishwashing, pricing the product affordably, and maintaining strict quality control.

Whatever else one could say about McDonald's food, it is eminently predictable. A Big Mac bought in Boston is indistinguishable from the same sandwich in Bangkok. It is so standardised that *The Economist* of London publishes an annual Big Mac Index to demonstrate the relative purchasing power of various currencies.

Some of the best and least expensive restaurants in the country are the small, independent operations run by recent immigrants. Cambodians, Chinese, Japanese, El Salvadorians, and Ethiopians bring their native dishes to add to the United States' already heady culinary stew. The great melting pot occasionally produces some odd restaurant bedfellows, such as Cuban-Vietnamese, Mex-Italian, or Hungarian-Puerto Rican.

Tea or Coffee

Americans drink coffee. Tea in most parts of the country means iced tea, specifically sweetened iced tea, and more specifically, sweetened iced tea with lemon. (The amount of sugar added generally increases as one heads south.)

Anyone who wants a cup of hot tea must be prepared to fight to get it. And even when one can be produced, it's guaranteed to be dreadful. The typical American tea service consists of a mug, paper cup, or little metal pot of hot water with a tea bag beside it. Sometimes a waiter will bring a box filled with different types of teas from which to choose. Ready-made hot tea is never served; Americans believe that when a restaurant pours boiling water directly over the tea in the kitchen it violates the customer's constitutional right to control the tea's strength.

Alcohol

On average, Americans consume more than 36 gallons (American gallons, naturally) of alcohol a year per person.

In most of the country (with the exception of Utah, which is full of teetotalling Mormons), it is perfectly legal and acceptable to have a drink. How and where it is served is another matter, because the sale and consumption of alcohol is regulated locally by states, counties, and towns. In some places one can drive up to a window and buy beer, even though drinking it in the car is illegal. In others places heavily guarded State Stores are only open during office hours and offer a minimal selection.

Root beer, in spite of its name, is not alcoholic. It's the American equivalent of ginger beer, but flavoured with sassafras and sarsparilla roots. Even Americans acknowledge that this is an acquired taste.

Traditional American beer is unique. It is not particularly good, just different from the beer the rest of the world drinks. One reason is the American climate: in the United States most beer is designed to be drunk in huge quantities, while watching sporting events, during weather hotter than 90°F. Hence the need for a high water content, to promote sweat, and a very low serving temperature, to prevent heatstroke. Too bad the cold kills what little taste the beer had in the first place. Dietary and safety concerns have married one another in the form of light beer, which is lower in calories, lower in alcohol, and (a truly awesome achievement) even lower in flavour than the usual beer.

In the past 15 years, however, a beer revolution has shaken America's brewing tradition to its foundations. Loosening of local alcohol laws has allowed some restaurants to brew their own beers on the premises, and nearly every city with any pretensions has at least one 'brewpub'. As a result, the number of breweries has more than doubled since 1987. This trend does lead to occasional lapses such as Christmas Cranberry Lager or Pumpkin Stout – but this is America.

Government and Bureaucracy

Government in America is like a layered pyramid. Over everything is the Federal government, which has certain responsibilities specified in the Constitution. Then there are 50 individual state governments which handle matters that are not allocated to the Federal government, such as education, liquor regulation, and automobile registration. Such laws can vary widely by state, leading, for example, to the flow of couples to the state where it's easiest to get divorced (Nevada).

States are subdivided into counties, which are divided into cities and townships. The bottom line is taxation: some US citizens must pay taxes to their city, county, state, and federal governments, and then try to live on anything left over.

Americans hate the very idea of government. Anti-government sentiment is what led the Colonies to split off on their own in the first place. "That government governs best that governs least", Americans will nod sagely to each other, or, similarly, "Keep the government's nose out of my business". This is a fine idea, as far as it goes. The only problem is, Americans love what government does.

They fight like bobcats if a Senator proposes a five-cent petrol tax, but they're happy as larks when the government repaves their exit from the freeway. They don't want the government to know about their medical problems or choose their doctor, but they really appreciate it when Uncle Jake, who fought in Korea, goes to the hospital for free because he's a veteran. They resent paying income tax, but Mom's social security check comes on time every month. Americans are irresolvably conflicted about their government. They want it to mind its own business, but they want it to do more for them. A lot of them would also like it to ban things of which they disapprove.

Structurally, the American national government has three branches: Legislative, Executive and Judicial. The bicameral Legislative branch, collectively called 'Congress', consists of the House of Representatives and the Senate.

Representatives are elected for two-year terms and serve a 'district'. (Each state is divided into voting districts according to population; thus Wyoming, a large but lightly populated state, has one district and one representative, whereas New Jersey, a small but populous state, has 13.) Representatives are expected to produce a certain amount of 'pork' for their district – government-funded highway projects, military installations and the like.

Each state also has two senators, regardless of population. Senators also need to bring home the bacon, but they are obligated to the entire state and only have to worry about being re-elected every six years.

Any American will tell you that Congress is a bunch of jackasses. The only exception is that person's own representative. Other congressmen who steer big government projects to their districts are playing 'pork barrel politics'. When one's own congressman does it, he's serving the constituency.

The president heads the Executive branch; he approves and ostensibly implements the laws passed by the legislature. In practice, the president and Congress spend most of their time blathering about how something might really be accomplished if the other weren't so obstinate.

The Judicial branch, in the person of the Supreme Court, has the ultimate authority over how and which laws are enforced. Thus, if Congress and the president enact a law that violates the Constitution, the Supreme Court can strike it down.

The genius of the whole system is that it is so cumbersome and complex that it has trouble accomplishing anything irredeemably stupid.

The Electoral College

Most Americans think that when they mark their ballot for a presidential candidate they have voted for that candidate. This is an illusion. They have actually cast a vote for the candidate's party. To choose the president, each state appoints a panel of electors equal in number to its senators and representatives, all from the winning party. Some six weeks after the popular election, these electors officially vote for President. Electors in most states are not obliged to vote for their state's winning candidate. It has happened that some electors voted for nobody, or for some other candidate, or even for the opposing candidate. This has never affected the result. Yet.

In an institution so arcane it is not surprising that things can go horribly awry. There have been four elections in which a presidential candidate won the popular vote yet lost the electoral college vote. This includes the 2000 presidential race. With Al Gore more than 300,000 votes ahead in the popular vote, George W. Bush was awarded Florida by a margin of 537 votes out of 6 million, or .009%. As a result, Bush had a majority in the Electoral College and got the presidency. (In an additional irony, Al Gore in his role as Vice President presided over the electoral college and thus certified his own defeat.)

In a purported democracy, the electoral college is about as un-democratic as you can get.

Systems

To apply the word 'system' to anything the Americans do is a bit optimistic. For example, the term 'health care system' masks the fact that the provision of health care in the United States is anything but systematic. Many people can't afford to go to the doctor or pay for private insurance. Then again, the 'criminal justice system' implies that criminals are treated fairly and justice is served, whereas anyone who has been involved with the courts knows that this is far from the truth.

The Americans' need to talk to each other means that the telephone system is the best in the world. Conversely, the American love for the automobile has driven all other forms of transportation into the ground, and the average city's public transport system is slow, inconvenient, and uncomfortable. In places like New York or Washington, however, it's still faster than driving.

One system that really works, or used to, in the United States is the highway system. When General Eisenhower was commanding the US forces in the European theatre, he saw Hitler's autobahns and said to himself, 'What a nifty way to move military equipment around the country. I wish America had such nice big roads.' Once he was president, he made his dream a reality. Thus was born the Interstate Highway System, now the atherosclerotic arteries of American commerce.

In the beginning, families would go for weekend drives and end the day by going to a drive-in restaurant so they could eat while still in their wonderful car. These days, suburban mothers battle through fierce traffic for hours as they shuttle their children from soccer practice to piano lessons, eating sandwiches behind the wheel out of sheer necessity.

A Little Learning is a Good Idea

Americans believe that going to college is a great idea and will qualify you for a better job, as long as you don't actually have to learn anything.

American lower education is divided into kindergarten, for the under-6 set, then grade school until age 12, then Junior High School for two years and then High School until around age 18.

State-run (public) schools vary enormously in quality depending upon the neighbourhood and the school taxes in each state. Fee-for-service (private) schools are patronised by parents who don't think the state-run schools are good enough for their children. The spectrum of private schools runs from elite institutions to splinter schools run by quirky ideologists or conservative religious groups.

To help lower-income parents, some municipalities issue vouchers that provide students with tuition in private schools. The one small problem with this is that courts have begun striking down such programs: vouchers may be used for religious schools, and this violates the Constitutional separation of church and state.

A university education is available to any American who can afford to pay the tuition and board (now totalling more than $26,000 per year at the major universities); who is needy, sporty or brainy enough to get a scholarship; or who is able to borrow the money. Borrowing the money is increasingly popular, and many students emerge from the university clutching their degree in one hand and the equivalent of a home mortgage repayment book in the other.

Nearly one-third of American secondary school students go on to university, but they don't fully trust what they learn there. Indeed, to the American public anyone who knows too much is suspect. Few Americans read, except for the occasional John Grisham or Robert Ludlum novel. Why bother? About the only subject an American office worker really needs to master is the rules of football.

Crime and Punishment

Americans are fiercely attached to the concept of individual rights, which are specifically spelled out in the country's constitution. These include freedoms of the press, of religion, and of public assembly; the right to be free from cruel and unusual punishment; and the right to keep and bear arms.

In the longstanding American tradition of taking a good idea to its most absurd extreme, these rights have been variously interpreted over the years as the right to publish detailed instructions for building an atomic bomb, the right to sacrifice chickens for religious purposes, the right to stage a political demonstration in support of Nazism, the right to watch television while incarcerated, and the right to order a Mannlicher-Carcano carbine through a mail-order catalogue. Trample on any of these rights and an American will raise an impressive stink, usually by filing a lawsuit.

A Nation of Lawyers

Since it's un-American to lose, no unfortunate event is ever the result of incompetence, or even bad luck. Americans shift the blame on to any handy object – their parents, the government, their spouses, the neighbours. Nothing is ever an American's own fault; therefore, any unfortunate event is grounds for a lawsuit. When an American suffers even a trivial embarrassment or misfortune, the first thought is not, "How can I live this down?" but rather, "I'll sue the bastards".

The desire to find someone to blame and then to 'sue the pants off them' has made the United States the most over-lawyered country in the world, with getting on for one million attorneys in a population of 275 million. The nation's capital has one lawyer for every 19 residents. This absurd situation occurs because laws are made, enforced, and reported on by lawyers. Congress includes nearly 400 lawyers, and thousands more clutter up government agencies, law enforcement, and the media.

Ridiculous lawsuits abound, including the man who jumped in front of a New York subway train and then sued for injury; the woman who sued the Pennsylvania state lottery because she did not win, and the golfer who sued a golf course when he was hit by his own ricocheting ball. In the United States, anyone can file a lawsuit, and often it seems as though just about everyone has.

Limiting Your Liabilities

In a litigious country like the United States, manufacturers try to limit their liability in every way possible, including warning consumers about possible ill effects from using their products. As a result, almost every product or device comes with a warning label of some sort. Carnival rides alert their riders 'May cause nausea'. Alcoholic beverages, cigarettes, and artificial sweeteners inform users about the substance's potential for cancer and birth defects. Laundry detergent advises 'Do not use internally', hair dryers warn 'Do not use in the shower', toasters caution 'Do not use on metal objects'.

The only possible explanation is that, coexisting with normal Americans is a species of humanoid lizards who toss their radios into the bathtub and put coins in their food processors. Unfortunately, even a casual reading of the average daily newspaper confirms this hypothesis.

Trial and Imprisonment

Under the American constitution, in theory criminals are innocent until proven guilty, are entitled to a speedy trial, may refuse to answer self-incriminating questions, and are entitled to representation by a lawyer. In practice, innocent means 'convicted in the newspapers but not in a court of law', speedy means 'before the accused dies of old age, unless he's pretty old already', and lawyer means 'now give that man in the pinstriped suit all your money'.

Since just about anything other than imprisonment is considered 'cruel and unusual punishment', convicted criminals go to jail. The United States has over a million of its citizens under lock and key – a higher incarceration rate than any other country in the world except Russia. At any given moment, 2.7% of the population are either in prison or on probation, a number equivalent to the entire population of Denmark.

It is gradually dawning on the average American that this kind of law enforcement is not only expensive, it doesn't work very well. But nobody knows what else to do about crime besides build more prisons. New facilities sprout like weeds as the old prisons fill up, and prison management is the new growth industry. In the meantime, crime continues unabated.

When an American police officer makes an arrest, he or she reads the so-called 'Miranda Warning', named after *Miranda v. State of Arizona*, the lawsuit that established that police must inform prisoners of their rights. When taking a suspected criminal into custody, the arresting officer must recite a lengthy warning which begins: 'You have the right to remain silent. If you give up the right to remain silent, anything you say can and will be used against you in a court of law...'

This by no means guarantees gentle treatment by the police. The quality of mercy meted out in the United States depends largely on the region of the country, the nature of the offence, and the attitude and identity of the purported perpetrator. When in doubt or in danger of arrest, a foreigner should say 'Yes, sir, officer' a lot, and wave a European passport.

Drug Use

An awful lot of people use drugs, even, perhaps especially, the rich. More than half of the nation's young adults admit to having used marijuana and nearly a fifth to having used cocaine. But it is still a tremendous solecism to talk publicly about one's drug use unless you are a recovering addict who wants to educate impressionable youth about their dangers.

Legal (i.e. prescription) drug use, on the other hand, is widespread and perfectly acceptable. In some circles it's customary to compare antidepressant dosages before moving on to other topics.

Bang, Bang

Approximately 25% of American households have at least one gun tucked away somewhere, and in the country as a whole there are an estimated 192 million guns. Gun ownership in the United States has the same legal backing as the right to vote and the right to a fair trial. Any attempt to regulate ownership of firearms precipitates a judicial crisis and draws shrieks of outrage from gun owners who fear that gun registration programmes and background checks will deprive them of their right to protect themselves. One of the country's most influential organisations, the 4.1 million-member National Rifle Association, has determinedly fought any and all attempts to restrict the free trade in firearms. Their reasoning is pretty well summed up by slogans like 'When guns are outlawed, only outlaws will have guns'.

Hunting remains one of the most popular American sports, with 15 million licensed hunters in the country, including the president. It's the sport of manly men, who wake before dawn to wander through the frosty woods or sit for hours in a bitterly cold duck blind and then go back to a cabin and drink heavily.

Most guns are owned by exactly such law-abiding citizens and are used carefully, but even these legal and respectable guns kill 31,000 Americans a year. In spite of what one might think, Americans are less likely to randomly shoot each other than to kill themselves (56% of all gun deaths are suicides). Children who find these guns tend to play with them, often with fatal results, and it has been proposed that schools have gun education, like sex education.

Some years ago a toy company manufactured a water gun called the Super Soaker which shoots a powerful stream of water for 50 feet. A group of teenagers playing with these got into an argument, and one was injured. The authorities in their town proposed regulating the water guns to prevent any further such incidents. They would not dream of proposing such legislation for guns that fire real bullets.

Business

Henry Ford didn't invent the automobile. Instead, he did something better, something even more American. He made cars cheap, cheap enough so that every family could afford one. His marketing philosophy was: 'They can have any colour they want, as long as it's black.'

These days what Americans want is choice – choice of colour, style, price and accessories. Successful entrepreneurs think in terms of 'niche marketing' and 'lateral extension' – in other words, providing more choice to increasingly individualised market segments. Car shoppers today can pick metalflake blue, fire-engine red, or any of a dozen other colours, with interiors to match.

The ultimate American concept is, of course, franchising – selling an already successful format to those who want to open a business. The result has been commercial homogenisation as Pizza Hut gobbles up restaurants and shopping precincts are taken over by The Gap and Victoria's Secret (which sells irresistible frothy underwear). An American's natural instinct is to take an already successful idea, improve on it, and then compete against the original. This creates an illusion of variety. Malls all have the same shops, department stores carry the same goods, and close examination reveals that products all contain the same ingredients. Thus Americans have vast freedom of choice, but it's between virtually indistinguishable options.

In the Office

Work, Americans feel, should be rewarding, interesting, and, if at all possible, fun. Play, on the other hand, requires dedication, persistence, skill and effort. No wonder Americans are confused. If the purpose of work is to succeed, and the purpose of play is to win, is there a difference? The bottom line for Americans is that work is defined as anything that earns money and play as anything that doesn't turn a profit.

This confusion extends to office attire and relationships. Waiters wear black tie, while software billionaires trot around in shorts and T-shirts with slogans on them. American offices grow increasingly relaxed: in a dot-com company where office amenities may include a tanning salon and a sauna, anything more than a swimsuit could be considered excessively formal.

For Americans, the distinction between a friend and a co-worker blurs to near invisibility. Around the office everyone, with the occasional exception of the company president, is called by his or her first name. Workers routinely discuss their personal affairs in the office, keeping each other informed about their home purchases, their children's illnesses, and the convoluted nature of their marital therapy.

American corporations contribute to the confusion by inviting business associates to social functions held outside business hours. The worst offences of this sort take place in Washington, DC, where the average congressman receives three or four invitations a day to cocktail receptions, lectures, charitable events, benefit dinners, and so forth, and where hostesses are measured not by how well their guests are entertained but by who shows up for the party.

The warm personal relationships Americans feel at work do not translate into strong corporate loyalty. Almost no-one stays with a corporation for his or her entire career. American workers will drop the present job for a better one without a moment's worry about what the change may mean for their employer because they have seen how loyal their employer is to them – to put it bluntly, not very. The profit motive drives all American commerce, and if staff cutbacks are required to maintain the balance sheet, a corporation will rarely show mercy in sending half the sales department out for a long walk.

Americans on the east and west coasts have strikingly different business styles. On the east coast, the goal is to appear to work as much as possible. Thus, in New York and Washington, employees, especially at law and publishing firms, stay on late into the evening and come into the offices on weekends. In Los Angeles the goal is to appear not to work at all, and deals worth hundreds of millions are discussed at the poolside. Neither coast does any more actual work than the other. Los Angeles continues to produce films and television, and New York keeps the stock market and corporate headquarters going, but both have the smug satisfaction of pointing to the other and saying, "See? We don't work ourselves to death/lie around on the beach wasting time like they do out on the East/West coast."

Language and Ideas

American speech is remarkably straightforward. They tell it as it is, even when it's not a particularly good idea to do so. Linguistic subtlety, innuendo, and irony that other nations find delightful puzzle the Americans, who take all statements at face value, weigh them for accuracy, and reject anything they don't understand. They call spades spades, or possibly 'earth-reorientation equipment' if they work for the government, and have trouble with complex metaphors.

The Americans' love of tinkering, of making things better, of including those who might be left out, and of avoiding negatives means that they view speaking English as just one more assimilation project. Words have been added from immigrants' languages (such as 'schmuck', a stupid or contemptible person), or conflated out of two words (such as 'brunch', a combination of br-eakfast and l-unch), or abbreviated and used for something only marginally related (such as 'nuke' for 'heat in a microwave oven'). Americans love new words and adopt them with alacrity. They also use them to death, as anyone who has had to listen to a business meeting about 'empowerment' can attest.

Slang

American idioms are colourful, varied and erratic, the sports-based ones particularly so.

Much of American slang derives from sport, such as avoiding the lines of authority by 'doing an end run', failing in an attempt by 'striking out', or taking on an easy task because it's a 'slam dunk'. Carrying on an ordinary sports conversation requires only a minimum of knowledge. A question such as, "Who do you favour for the big one?" works well, especially in early January, as does the comment, "How about them Dodgers/Steelers/Bullets/Broncos/Yankees/Falcons/Bears/Eagles/Red Sox?" Suitable post-game comments include "If you ask me, there were some pretty funny calls in that game", or "A good team makes its own breaks". These work for almost any sport except possibly chess or bridge.

Learning American slang, or indeed any slang, is shooting at a moving target. Teenagers and technology constantly create new words and new uses for old words. For example, 'burn' can now mean 'copy', as in "burn me a CD of that new game, willya?" Local slang spreads rapidly through television, movies, and the Internet, so formerly arcane terms like the New York 'skanky' (unsavoury, disgusting) become commonplace country-wide. Fortunately slang becomes obsolete rapidly, so there's very little point in trying to keep up.

Let's Verb Nouns

In the United States no noun is too proper to use as a verb. "We're trialing that now", says a company spokes-woman about a new service. "It's impacted our options", says a politician about a setback his campaign has suffered. "We obsolete our products", says Bill Gates about Microsoft's manufacturing policy.

Verbs are action words, much nicer than stolid, immovable nouns. Since most Americans can't name the parts of speech anyway, they use them interchangeably.

Political Correctness

In almost all circumstances discrimination on the basis of race, religion, or sex is not permitted. All-male and all-white clubs have toppled like dominoes under threats of legal action. Besides, minorities and women have money, and every organisation appreciates members who can afford the dues.

Political correctness now debates the worthiness of many words. The worst word of all, one that should never be used under any circumstances, is the racial epithet beginning with 'n', unless the speaker actually is one. Words referring to body functions are polite by comparison.

Hundreds of euphemisms have sprung up to cope with politically incorrect vocabulary. The handicapped are now 'mobility-challenged', the blind 'perceptually impaired' and the not so bright 'knowledge-base non-possessors'. People don't have pets, they have 'companion animals'. Nor are they short or fat, but 'vertically challenged' or 'persons of size'. No-one has a failure, he or she has a 'deficiency rating'.

The American language embraces the bias towards good feelings. Someone doesn't have a near brush with death; he or she has a 'life-affirming experience'. Stocks that plummet to half their value are not losers, they are 'non-performers'. Applicants who do not receive a job offer are 'selected out'. An upbeat business vernacular calls every problem a 'challenge' and every massive lay-off 'rightsizing'. Mindless cheerfulness particularly pervades the real estate profession, in which 'cosy' is code for 'smaller than a refrigerator carton' and 'country charm' means 'no retail establishments within walking distance'. Disney theme parks are special hotbeds of such optimism, with perky, well-groomed employees who do nothing but smile, smile, smile.

All this boundless good nature can grate on visitors from more reserved nations. It's enough to give a European a de-enhanced attitude.

The Author

Stephanie Faul lives in Washington, DC, where she works in public relations as a 'talking head'. Growing up in the nation's capital has given her a unique perspective on the foibles and quirks of her compatriots and has confirmed her belief in Bismarck's remark that laws are like sausages: it's better not to see them being made.

Ms Faul is a typical product of American hybrid vigour: she is half Czech immigrant, half Connecticut Yankee, with a German-speaking grandmother and cousins in Canada, England and Switzerland. Her xenophobic perceptions were honed in a French primary school, a Swiss boarding school, college summers spent drinking Newcastle Brown Ale in British pubs, and occasional trips to Asia and Florida. At home she enjoys African music, Vietnamese food, Italian footwear, Siamese cats, and English novels.

In many ways she feels typically American – curious, inventive, outspoken and practical – but atypical attributes include a distaste for shopping and television and a marked preference for walking instead of driving, which in her neighbourhood is usually faster anyway. Her current ambition is to visit all 50 US states. She has only a dozen left to go, but at a walking pace this could take some time.